Table of Contents

As we embark on this comprehensive journey, each chapter contributes to a holistic understanding of men's mental health, aiming to foster a world where every man feels supported, understood, and empowered in their mental well-being.

Chapter 1: Unveiling the Depths: A Journey into Men's Mental Health

In the intricate tapestry of human experience, the threads of mental health are woven into every aspect of our lives. However, when it comes to understanding men's mental health, there exists a mosaic of complexities that demand our attention and empathy. In this chapter, we embark on a profound exploration of the unique challenges and nuances that shape the mental well-being of men.

1.1 Breaking the Silence

For far too long, a pervasive silence has shrouded men's mental health. Societal expectations and gender norms often dictate that men should embody strength, resilience, and emotional stoicism. The unwritten code of masculinity, handed down through generations, has contributed to the stigma surrounding mental health issues in men.

This chapter seeks to unravel the layers of this silence and encourages an open dialogue about the psychological well-being of men.

1.2 The Mask of Masculinity

In the quest to conform to societal expectations, men often wear a metaphorical mask, concealing their vulnerabilities behind a façade of toughness. Breaking through this mask requires a deep understanding of the internal struggles men face. From the pressure to be the primary breadwinner to the expectations of unyielding emotional strength, these societal norms shape the mental health narrative for men.

1.3 The Impact of Cultural and Societal Expectations

Culture plays a pivotal role in shaping our perceptions of mental health. Different societies impose varying expectations on men, influencing how they perceive and express their emotions. Exploring these cultural influences provides insight into the diverse ways men experience mental health challenges and seek help.

1.4 Navigating Emotional Terrain

Men, like all individuals, navigate a vast emotional terrain. Understanding the intricacies of male emotions requires dismantling stereotypes that portray men as emotionally distant or unresponsive. By acknowledging the full spectrum of emotions, we pave the way for a more comprehensive understanding of men's mental health.

1.5 The Intersectionality of Men's Mental Health

Recognizing that men's mental health is not a one-size-fits-all concept, we delve into the intersectionality that colours each man's experience. Factors such as race, sexual orientation, socioeconomic status, and age intersect with gender to create a unique tapestry of mental health challenges. This chapter sheds light on the importance of considering these intersections in addressing the diverse needs of men.

1.6 The Call for Empathy and Support

As we embark on this exploration, it becomes evident that dismantling stereotypes, breaking the silence, and understanding the complexities of men's mental health require a collective effort. This chapter sets the stage for a broader conversation, urging society to approach men's mental health with empathy, compassion, and a commitment to fostering environments where men feel safe to express their struggles and seek help.

In the chapters that follow, we will journey deeper into the specific challenges faced by men, exploring the impact of societal expectations, examining prevalent mental health issues, and proposing strategies for cultivating a culture of mental well-being that embraces and supports men on their unique paths to emotional fulfilment.

Chapter 2: Deconstructing Societal Norms

In the intricate dance of societal expectations, men find themselves bound by a set of norms that have long dictated their roles, behaviours, and expressions. This chapter delves into the layers of these norms, exploring their impact on men's mental health and advocating for a redefinition of masculinity that promotes well-being.

2.1 The Pressure to Conform

Societal expectations often cast men into predefined roles, pressuring them to conform to traditional notions of masculinity. This section examines how these expectations shape identity, perpetuating a narrow definition of what it means to be a man. The chapter explores the toll this conformity takes on men's mental health, as they grapple with the internal conflict between societal expectations and personal authenticity.

2.2 Redefining Masculinity

As we navigate the challenges posed by societal norms, the need for redefining masculinity becomes apparent. This section advocates for a broader, more inclusive definition—one that allows men the freedom to express their full range of emotions, strengths, and vulnerabilities. Redefining masculinity is not about diminishing strength but embracing the strength found in authenticity and emotional intelligence.

2.3 Toxic Masculinity's Toll on Mental Health

Toxic masculinity, characterised by rigid gender norms, dominance, and the suppression of vulnerability, can have severe consequences on men's mental well-being. This part of the chapter examines the roots and manifestations of toxic masculinity, dissecting how it contributes to mental health issues such as anxiety, depression, and emotional detachment.

2.4 The Role of Media and Popular Culture

Media and popular culture play a significant role in perpetuating societal norms and shaping perceptions of masculinity. This section analyses how portrayals of men in movies, television, and advertising contribute to unrealistic expectations. It also explores how media can be a powerful tool for change, challenging stereotypes and promoting positive narratives surrounding men's mental health.

2.5 Celebrating Vulnerability

In a world that often equates vulnerability with weakness, this section encourages a paradigm shift. Vulnerability is not a flaw but a strength—a key to authentic connection and emotional well-being. The chapter concludes by exploring ways to celebrate vulnerability, both on an individual level and as a society, fostering environments where men feel empowered to express their true selves without fear of judgement.

As we unravel the layers of societal norms in this chapter, the goal is to pave the way for a more compassionate and accepting understanding of masculinity. By deconstructing these norms, we open a space for men to navigate their identities authentically, ultimately contributing to improved mental health and a more inclusive society.

Chapter 3: Common Mental Health Challenges in Men

Within the intricate tapestry of men's mental health, certain challenges emerge as recurrent threads that demand our attention. This chapter delves into the nuanced landscape of common mental health issues affecting men, shedding light on the complexities and impact these challenges have on their well-being.

3.1 Depression and Anxiety

The silent companions of many men, depression and anxiety weave through their lives, often unnoticed or unspoken. This section explores the manifestation of these mental health challenges in men, acknowledging the unique ways they may present and the societal factors that contribute to their prevalence. It also emphasises the importance of recognizing and addressing these issues to break the cycle of silent suffering.

3.2 Substance Abuse and Dependency

As a coping mechanism or an attempt to drown inner turmoil, substance abuse is a prevalent issue among men. This part of the chapter examines the relationship between mental health struggles and substance abuse, unravelling the interconnected web that often traps individuals in a cycle of dependency. Strategies for intervention, rehabilitation, and prevention are also discussed.

3.3 Suicide and Suicidal Ideation

In the darkest corners of mental health, the specter of suicide looms large. This section bravely confronts the reality of suicide and suicidal ideation among men. It addresses the societal stigma that often surrounds these issues and emphasizes the importance of destigmatizing conversations about suicide, fostering awareness, and providing support for those at risk.

3.4 Post-Traumatic Stress Disorder (PTSD)

Men, particularly those who have served in the military or experienced trauma, may grapple with Post-Traumatic Stress Disorder. This part of the chapter explores the unique challenges faced by men dealing with PTSD, including the stigma associated with seeking help and the impact on personal relationships. Strategies for creating supportive environments and effective therapeutic interventions are also discussed.

3.5 Work-related Stress and Burnout

In a society that often ties self-worth to professional success, work-related stress and burnout are common foes of men's mental health. This section investigates the toll that demanding careers, high expectations, and a relentless pursuit of success can take on mental well-being. It advocates for a holistic approach to work-life balance and explores strategies for preventing and mitigating workplace stress.

As we navigate the landscapes of these common mental health challenges, this chapter seeks to foster understanding and empathy. By confronting these issues head-on, we pave the way for meaningful conversations, support systems, and interventions that can contribute to a healthier mental well-being for men across diverse backgrounds and experiences.

Chapter 4: Seeking Help: Breaking the Barriers

In the labyrinth of men's mental health, the pathway to healing is often obstructed by formidable barriers. This chapter illuminates the challenges men face in seeking help, dismantles the stigma surrounding mental health support, and advocates for a culture that encourages open conversations and professional intervention.

4.1 Overcoming Stigma

Stigma remains a formidable foe in the realm of men's mental health. This section explores the pervasive stigma that discourages men from seeking help, examining the roots of societal judgement and dispelling misconceptions. Strategies for challenging and dismantling stigma are discussed, paving the way for a more understanding and supportive community.

4.2 Encouraging Open Conversations

Breaking the silence requires the courage to engage in open and honest conversations about mental health. This part of the chapter explores the power of dialogue in normalising discussions around mental well-being. It provides guidance on fostering communication within families, friendships, and communities, creating spaces where men feel safe to share their struggles without fear of judgement.

4.3 The Importance of Professional Support

Navigating the complexities of mental health often necessitates professional guidance. This section underscores the significance of seeking help from mental health professionals, offering insights into the variety of therapeutic interventions available. It addresses common hesitations men may have about counselling, emphasising the transformative potential of therapy in fostering emotional resilience and well-being.

4.4 Building Supportive Communities

No man is an island, and building supportive communities is essential in the journey toward mental health. This part of the chapter explores the role of community organisations, peer support groups, and online platforms in creating spaces where men can connect, share experiences, and access resources. It advocates for the power of communal support in breaking down isolation and fostering a sense of belonging.

4.5 Integrating Mental Health into Primary Care

This section advocates for the integration of mental health into routine healthcare, emphasising the importance of holistic well-being. It explores how primary care providers can play a pivotal role in identifying and addressing mental health concerns, breaking down the barriers that often separate physical and mental health. The chapter concludes with a call to action for a more comprehensive and integrated approach to healthcare.

As we navigate the challenges of seeking help, this chapter aims to dismantle the barriers that hinder men from accessing the support they need. By fostering a culture that encourages open conversations, normalises seeking professional help, and builds supportive communities, we pave the way for a future where men can embark on their mental health journey with courage, resilience, and the assurance that they are not alone.

Chapter 5: Cultivating Emotional Intelligence

In the intricate landscape of men's mental health, emotional intelligence emerges as a guiding compass. This chapter delves into the profound significance of understanding and navigating emotions, advocating for a paradigm shift that empowers men to cultivate emotional resilience and forge authentic connections.

5.1 Understanding Emotional Literacy

The journey to robust mental health begins with understanding the language of emotions. This section explores the concept of emotional literacy, emphasising the importance of recognizing, expressing, and interpreting emotions. It provides practical strategies for developing emotional intelligence and dispels the notion that certain emotions are incompatible with masculinity.

5.2 Teaching Emotional Resilience

Emotional resilience is the armour that shields against life's inevitable challenges. This part of the chapter delves into the cultivation of emotional resilience, offering insights into coping mechanisms, stress management, and the importance of embracing vulnerability as a source of strength. It advocates for a proactive approach to mental well-being that equips men with the tools to navigate life's ups and downs.

5.3 Fostering Healthy Communication

Effective communication is the bridge that connects individuals, fostering understanding and connection. This section explores the role of communication in men's mental health, highlighting the benefits of open and honest dialogue. It provides practical tips for expressing emotions, active listening, and navigating difficult conversations, paving the way for healthier relationships and improved mental well-being.

5.4 Empathy as a Path to Connection

Empathy, the ability to understand and share the feelings of others, emerges as a powerful force in cultivating meaningful connections. This part of the chapter delves into the role of empathy in men's mental health, emphasising its transformative impact on relationships and personal well-being. It advocates for the practice of empathy as a cornerstone of emotional intelligence.

5.5 The Role of Education in Emotional Well-being

Education becomes a catalyst for change, shaping perceptions and fostering understanding. This section explores the role of education in promoting emotional well-being, advocating for comprehensive mental health education at various levels. It emphasises the need for destigmatizing emotions, teaching coping skills, and fostering a culture that prioritises emotional intelligence.

As we navigate the depths of emotional intelligence, this chapter seeks to empower men with the tools and knowledge needed to embrace their emotions authentically. By fostering emotional literacy, resilience, and healthy communication, we pave the way for a future where men navigate their emotional landscapes with confidence, forging connections that contribute to a robust and resilient mental well-being.

Chapter 6: Empowering Men Through Intersectionality

The mosaic of men's mental health is enriched by the intersectionality of diverse experiences. In this chapter, we explore the nuanced intersections of identity, acknowledging that the challenges faced by men are influenced by factors such as race, sexual orientation, socioeconomic status, and age.

6.1 Recognizing Diverse Experiences

Men's mental health is not a monolithic experience but a tapestry woven with threads of diverse identities. This section delves into the importance of recognizing and understanding the diverse experiences of men. It explores how factors such as race, ethnicity, cultural background, and personal history intersect with gender to shape unique mental health narratives.

6.2 Addressing Racial and Ethnic Disparities

Race and ethnicity play a significant role in shaping mental health experiences. This part of the chapter examines the impact of systemic racism, discrimination, and cultural factors on the mental well-being of men from diverse racial and ethnic backgrounds. It advocates for culturally sensitive mental health approaches and interventions that address disparities in access and treatment.

6.3 LGBTQ+ Perspectives on Men's Mental Health

Men within the LGBTQ+ community navigate distinct challenges that intersect with their gender identity and sexual orientation. This section explores the unique mental health considerations faced by gay, bisexual, transgender, and queer men. It emphasises the importance of creating inclusive and affirming spaces that validate diverse identities.

6.4 Socioeconomic Factors and Access to Resources

Socioeconomic status significantly influences the mental health landscape. This part of the chapter delves into the impact of financial stability, employment opportunities, and access to resources on men's mental well-being. It advocates for addressing socioeconomic disparities and creating equitable pathways to mental health support.

6.5 Age-Related Challenges

As men progress through different life stages, their mental health needs evolve. This section explores the challenges faced by men at various ages, from adolescence to midlife and beyond. It highlights the importance of age-appropriate interventions and support systems that address the unique mental health considerations associated with different life stages.

By acknowledging and embracing the intersectionality of men's mental health, this chapter seeks to foster inclusivity and understanding. It advocates for tailored approaches that honour the diversity of men's experiences, ensuring that mental health initiatives are culturally competent, affirming, and responsive to the multifaceted nature of identity.

Chapter 7: Creating Supportive Environments

In the pursuit of men's mental health, the creation of supportive environments is paramount. This chapter explores the integral role played by workplaces, educational institutions, families, and communities in fostering a culture that prioritises mental well-being and provides avenues for support.

7.1 Workplace Initiatives for Mental Health

The workplace, often a significant aspect of a man's life, can be a source of stress or a pillar of support. This section delves into the importance of workplace initiatives for mental health, advocating for policies that promote a healthy work-life balance, reduce stigma, and provide resources for mental well-being. It explores the benefits of fostering a supportive organisational culture that prioritises the mental health of employees.

7.2 Educational Programs and Awareness Campaigns

Education serves as a powerful tool in shaping attitudes and perceptions. This part of the chapter emphasises the role of educational programs and awareness campaigns in dismantling stigma and promoting mental health literacy. It explores the implementation of mental health education in schools and universities, aiming to equip individuals with the knowledge and skills needed to support themselves and others.

7.3 Community Outreach and Resources

Communities play a pivotal role in shaping the well-being of their members. This section explores the importance of community outreach and resources in creating supportive environments. It advocates for the development of accessible mental health resources, community-led support groups, and initiatives that foster connection and solidarity among residents.

7.4 Family and Relationship Dynamics

The family unit serves as a foundational element in men's lives. This part of the chapter delves into the dynamics of family relationships and their impact on men's mental health. It explores strategies for promoting open communication, breaking down generational patterns of silence, and creating familial environments that support emotional expression and vulnerability.

7.5 The Role of Government and Policy

Government policies play a crucial role in shaping the landscape of mental health. This section examines the impact of public policies on men's mental health, advocating for initiatives that prioritise mental health funding, reduce disparities in access to care, and promote mental health as an integral component of public health.

As we navigate the various environments influencing men's mental health, this chapter aims to inspire actionable steps towards fostering supportive and nurturing spaces.

By recognizing the significance of workplaces, educational institutions, communities, families, and governmental policies, we lay the foundation for a holistic approach to mental well-being that transcends individual efforts and contributes to a culture of collective support.

Chapter 8: Moving Forward: A Blueprint for Change

In the culmination of our exploration into men's mental health, this chapter serves as a call to action, providing a blueprint for change. It outlines strategies for advocacy, continued research, global perspectives, and personal and collective responsibility, paving the way for a future where men's mental health is prioritised and supported.

8.1 Advocacy and Activism

Advocacy and activism serve as catalysts for societal change. This section explores the role of individuals, organisations, and communities in advocating for men's mental health. It discusses the importance of challenging societal norms, promoting awareness, and actively participating in initiatives that seek to destigmatize mental health and create supportive environments.

8.2 Research and Continued Understanding

The pursuit of knowledge is a cornerstone in addressing the complexities of men's mental health. This part of the chapter emphasises the need for continued research to deepen our understanding of the unique challenges men face. It advocates for research initiatives that explore intersectionality, cultural influences, and evolving patterns in men's mental health, informing evidence-based interventions and policies.

8.3 Global Perspectives on Men's Mental Health

Men's mental health is a global concern that requires a broad perspective. This section examines the impact of cultural, social, and economic factors on men's mental health globally. It advocates for cross-cultural dialogue, the exchange of best practices, and the development of global initiatives that recognize and address the diverse needs of men around the world.

8.4 Personal and Collective Responsibility

Change begins at an individual level and extends to collective responsibility. This part of the chapter encourages individuals to take responsibility for their mental well-being and encourages communities to foster a culture of collective support. It explores the power of interpersonal connections and emphasises the role of each person in contributing to a society that values and prioritises men's mental health.

8.5 A Vision for a Mentally Healthy Future

The final section of the chapter paints a vision for a mentally healthy future. It envisions a world where men feel empowered to express their emotions freely, where mental health is prioritised in every aspect of life, and where societal norms are inclusive and affirming. It calls for a collective commitment to creating a future where men's mental health is not only understood but actively supported.
As we conclude this journey through the intricate layers of men's mental health, this chapter sets the stage for a proactive and transformative approach. By engaging in advocacy, supporting continued research, fostering global perspectives, taking personal and collective responsibility, and envisioning a mentally healthy future, we lay the groundwork for a world where every man can thrive emotionally and contribute to a more compassionate and understanding society

www.ingramcontent.com/pod-product-compliance
Lightning Source LLC
Chambersburg PA
CBHW060910260726
48661CB00008B/3569